Leaving the Mickey

Patricia Irvine lives on Adelaide's Le Fevre Peninsula. A former secondary teacher, she is an enthusiastic paddler who operated a kayak ecotour business in the local mangroves for many years. She is now studying for the Advanced Diploma of Arts (Professional Writing) at Adelaide Institute of TAFE.

In the past four years she has won several poetry contests and a nature writing contest. She has performed on 5UV 'Writers' Radio' and on ABC 891. A number of her poems have been broadcast on ABC Radio National's PoeticA.

She has just finished a book adaptation for ABC Radio National's First Person.

She has published articles on ornithology and mangrove ecology, and has had a script accepted by ABC Radio National's 'Science Show'. Her interests include surfing, weight training and birdwatching. She loves aerial sports – she's a former diver and trampolinist, and has 987 parachute jumps and 350 hours of gliding.

Leaving the Mickey

Patricia Irvine

Friendly Street Poets

Wakefield Press

Friendly Street Poets Incorporated
in association with
Wakefield Press
1 The Parade West
Kent Town
South Australia 5067

www.friendlystreetpoets.org.au
www.wakefieldpress.com.au

First published 2004
Copyright © Patricia Irvine, 2004

Cover illustration by John Hilliard
Cover artwork by Vicki Whitcomb
Text designed and typeset by Clinton Ellicott
Printed and bound by Hyde Park Press

National Library of Australia
Cataloguing-in-publication entry

Irvine, Patricia.
Leaving the mickey.

ISBN 1 86254 635 5.

I. Title.

A821.4

Wakefield Press thanks Fox Creek Wines
and Arts South Australia for their support.

The manuscript of this book was written as part of the Advanced Diploma
of Arts (Professional Writing) at the Adelaide Institute of TAFE.

Dedicated to

Robert David Irvine
5/5/1945–24/1/1997
who said,
'Shut up – you're embarrassing me!'

Contents

I

Black Box

Catholic Girls' Skipping Song 1959

Pellegrini,
jellybeanie.
Mortal sin's a
brief bikini.
Sugar Stations
of the Cross.
St Therese and fairy floss.
Nine First Fridays,
rosary beads,
first confession,
calloused knees.
Missals, veils and scapulars,
relics, penance, Christmas stars.
Parish bingo. SP bookie.
What's a condom? What's a nookie?
Convent schools are always best;
public schools don't pass the test.
Candles, incense, Latin, lace,
keep us in a state of grace.
Don't commit adultery.
Skip until it's time for tea.

Black Box

Father O'Who in the Tardis
slid the panel back –
a doggy door for sin
that wriggled through the grille
of the black box vice recorder.

Keeper of secret shames,
I told you all.
Hail, holy phonebox,
hotline to forgiveness!

Seven: the age of reason.
Old enough to sin.
Watched by the plaster man on the cross,
my list compiled, rehearsed – it never changed –
I joined the queue for the sacred laundromat.
Ecce homo washes whiter ...

Absolvo te. My washing done,
I left in smug relief
to patter through my penance.
Three Hail Marys; no more original
than the sins I'd confessed,
that arced away, returned
for next week's matinee:

I said 'bugger' and 'bum'.
I was cheeky to mum
But I made a short Act of Contrition,
and I could spell it!
And other big words:
heresy   adultery   apostasy
redemption   incarnation   assumption.

Dogma?
A pushover!

From Bowdler to the Beatles
A memoir of a Catholic education.

1960–64.
We're in the Menzies era.
Blacks are neither seen nor heard
except for Namatjira.

1960. Pretty City.
Athens on the Torrens.
Festival of Arts and Flowers.
Could have been in Florence.

Wriggling sprogs in summer heat
jampacked in the City Baths.   *The narrator exposes the tyrannical school rules.*
Hindley Street and Rundle Street
were both forbidden paths.

Hair cut short above our collars
(or it *could* be done in plaits!)
Gloves; suspenders; pounds, not dollars.
Rebels wore rope petticoats.

Little smarties threw mixed parties,
though our mums had all signed cards
vowing that stray prospecting males
should never sully our backyards.

Girls seen smoking, eyeing schoolboys
–('I was most disedified!')–   *The Principal's constant refrain.*
Summer hats ironed flat like boaters;
berets stuffed with scarves inside:

was this mortal sin or venial
or only an occasion?
New Australians in our class;
sometimes a token Asian.

The poet acquaints the uninformed with the
subtleties of canon law & theology . . .

Catholic girls got Catholic schooling.
Meat on Friday was a sin.
It was okay for *non*-Catholics:
they were OUT but we were IN!

Mothers' Club and Fathers' Club
were discrete and segregated.
Did the management believe
none of them had copulated?

. . . and observes the social strictures of
the period . . .

Father was the one who worked.
Mother stayed at home,
Mr Sheening laminex
and chatting on the phone.

Anomalous the widow's child.
Mum was our breadwinner.
Better boring factory work
than empty plates at dinner.

. . . and the alienation of the deviant.

Early 60s. Anglo city.
Flower clock in Victoria Square.
Pizza parlour called Marina's.
Baby, I was there!

The poet observes the cultural infiltration of the
Mediterranean & admits complicity.

There were token New Australians
we accepted as our own:
Latin fish shops, Greek greengrocers,
thinly spread to keep up tone.

Cappuccino at Sigalas'.
– ('I was most disedified!') –
Perry Como on the wireless
in the days before Gay Pride.

Beehives sprayed rock-hard with lacquer
so they wouldn't dent or bend;
wearers perving on Nureyev's
shapely legs and nether end.

Cautionary, apocryphal,
breathlessly we circulated
the story of a beehive dome
in which a cockroach clan had mated.

1964: The Beatles.   *She participates in the event of the century ...*
Giant queue down Gawler Place
for a ticket, bought at Allan's.
'Here's a pound! Please save my place!'

Parents knew when they were beaten.
Kids were sleeping in the street.
John and Paul and George and Ringo
made the powers that were retreat.

Prefects tried to round us up,
playing hard at Queen Canute.
Civil disobedience
had grown an Aloysian root.

'We shall not be moved!' we cried.
One girl you could punish,
but fifty soon become immune
from all the strictures of the nunnish.

Such trivial disobedience
– *I wanna hold your hand* –
gave us the raw ingredients
to protest over Vietnam,
the gerrymander, all-male bars,
race and sex discrimination.
Those who could abandoned bras,
to decent people's consternation.

Sit-ins, marches, mini-skirts
saw us through the sixties.
I'm widowed, fat and fifty-four.
Who'll restore youth's sweet elixirs?

*... & ponders the political implications of
her actions.*

*A sadder & a wider dame
She rose the morrow morn.*

Widow's Peak

Mustaghata, Kongur, Annapurna, Everest:
the last four steps of my solo ascent
to the ladder's apex, the metal A
that scores a point off gravity.

Fluoro tube in one hand,
starter in my mouth,
I teeter, mumble widowspeak.
For
since the hearse took my tall man
three weeks after his last ascent
of this domestic peak
I've feared the lonely climb –
twelve foot ceiling,
flush light fitting. An inch to go.
I strain,
        tiptoe,
                and miss.

                        Outside,
two honeyeaters train
on a bottlebrush trapeze.
Gymnasts, they spin,
sip sports drinks, sing.
If I fall their song will be
my Dies Irae.
                One last try.

Send me Sherpas, pitons, axes.
Two short acrobats, piggybacked,
could make this pitch.

<pre>
                        Not I.
I shy from danger, pray
for a tall dark stranger.

The doorbell. Goody Twosuits! Questing Mormons!
Lanky young Elders! Bet they're basketballers.
Callers, welcome. Come into my parlour.
Mount my ladder, push my starter, probe
that hard-to-get-at crevice.

                        Come again,
travelling evangelists, holy mountain men.
</pre>

Mammogram

Welcome to the Women's Biennale,
to the Tate for tit,
to the Westfield Wing
of the Cancer Cathedral.

No neophyte,
I know the rubrics:

strip to the waist,
step to the altar,
offer up your breasts
to the god in the machine,
singly on the plate.

Wince at your captive breast,
a specimen in a botanist's press.
(And does a plant feel pain, unease?)
Breathe in and hold . . .
Turn 90 degrees.
Same breast but
sideways squeeze.

Other tit.
Same shit.
Back to the cubicle.
On with the kit.

Pray I don't catch the jury's eye.
Hope that I won't be hung
or win a booby prize –
tinned crab, a can of worms.
Better to avoid the short list.
Better no Second Coming
for a Last Judgement.

Launching from Bingen

Hail, holy Hildegard,
pure Gothic rocket
of kevlar and ivory, silk and titanium,
wild as uranium.
Reach towards Byzantium.
Touch the apocalypse,
sharp, fiery diamond.

Slip through the filter of your stained-glass museum.
Smash your stained slide in the holy laboratory.
Break your spired gantry and rise over Rupertsburg,
freighted with visions of the world as a web
spun across centuries, continents, consciousness.

Entrained in your vapour
we surf on your wake
the great standing wave of earth orbit.

Cinctured in LEO, swung bullroarers singing,
we swathe through the stratosphere,
carve the ionosphere,
read the tattoos on the skin of the planet:
the dove on the sill,
the lily and the thorn,
the honeyeater's probe in the kangaroo paw,
bare-arsed Pythagoras, the emperor disrobed,
sunstruck and reeling on the edge of Lake Frome.
The gibber's a carapace – ochre and ash –
and frilled lizard tracks us with his satellite dish.

Looping in LEO over dot-painted deserts
and marblings of mountains aswirl under cloud,
higher than eagles your signature's arcing:
a breath of boronia, an offering of incense.

Notes
Hildegard of Bingen (1098–1179) was a Benedictine nun,
a visionary, mystic, poet, composer, theologian, natural
scientist and preacher. She was an extraordinarily powerful
and influential woman. Her heart and tongue are preserved in
the parish church at Rudesheim on the Rhine. Rupertsburg is
the name of the convent she founded at Bingen. LEO is the
rocket scientist's abbreviation for the term Low Earth Orbit.

Crumpled Tissue

'... *When man dies*
the wardrobe gapes instead.
We acquire the idle state
of your jackets and ties.'
Joseph Brodsky, *Elegy: for Robert Lowell.*

An archaeology of a recent past,
this suitcase open on our bed.
Why do I excavate?
Why tinker with these shards
now you have gone?

Why do I clutch your dirty shirts and underwear
as though they were the man? Why do I weep
as your sweat rises
live as Lazarus,
a holy incense?
I've mocked the cult of relics,
sneered at peasant pieties.
What else is left me now?

This grubby denim maps your body's postures
in faded blue demotic.
Rigid with grime,
knees and seat rubbed pale,
pockets scarred with memories of their cargo –
your keys, loose change, a few small nuts and bolts,
a crumpled tissue. Commonplace, domestic.
I check from habit.

But you are three days dead,
offal and shattered bone,
detritus on a mortuary slab,
the jigsaw no pathologist can solve –
smashed urn, ruined city,
this mass of crumpled tissue that I loved.

Boccia Player, Paralympics 2000

Hawking on speed,
he writhes
as if an earthquake rolled beneath his clay.
Centred in a Flemish frame,
caged in a Bosch inferno,
he dances to mad anarchy's clashed cymbals.

Cold puppeteers compete.
One yanks his left arm up and back; his rival
jerks it down. They brawl for custody.

The puppet snaps his strings,
plays solo.

His left arm hoists his right.
Hand cupped above his shoulder,
he takes the ball in reverence,
a communicant at the sacrament of sport.

His face, transfigured, is
a Breugel reveller's,
as ball
finds jack.

The Diver

Her foot adjusts the fulcrum,
reading its knurled braille wheel.
Her toes twitch on the springboard's skid-proof grit.
Her heart assaults the palings of her ribs.
Three times she breathes, exhales,
calls heart to heel, and steps, the first of four.
Ripple and flex of metal, steady as meditation,
impels her to the hurdle step,
the drop, the taut-strung launch.

Then, crimped in an N, a jumping-jack,
fingers grip shins, calves squeezed to thighs.
In a fury of hip-snap
heels chase head
round their living axle
till her piked flare
brakes
the spin.

Stretch, rip, deceive the surface
with tense hooked fists.
She slits the blue,
meets bubble-rush and tickle.
The whoosh of water gravels in her ears.

In a squat on the pool's blue floor,
crushed under fluid tonnes,
she presses once,
erupts
to light and breath,
in lycra metaphor of womanflesh.

Alzheimer's Fugue

In Britain it carries away 100,000 minds a year.
A planeload a day. One every five minutes.
'Assault on the mind: the battle against
Alzheimer's Disease.' (Channel Four, London).

Unwitting, you board your last flight.
You think you are safely at home
as you sit in your easy chair.

The gas ring, left on overnight,
fires up your solo balloon,
gashing the dark with its flare.

You leave without documentation
on your international flight.
Your life's been a declination

to this slow and silent translation:
the self flown high as a kite.
Thinner and colder the air

round your bubble, light-bulb, balloon –
the symbol of thought in cartoon.
You filter your way through pale starlight,
past the hammocking curve of the moon.

In daylight we see how you dangle,
silent, confused and distraught,
above the Bemusing Triangle,
to the west of the Cape of Good Thought,

to sag in a heap on a dune
at the edge of a beach. The berm

is crumbling, the ocean wild,
and you are all alone.

On the narrow shore of reason
it is matter over mind
as high tide has its season.

Pia mater, pray for us,
dura mater, shield us.
Protect this fragile globe,
this softly crinkled world
we carry each within us.
Pia mater, gentle mother,
stay within my reach,
lest I become the next shell
cast empty on the beach.

Semaphore Sunday

I wake when sun drips syrup on my pane.
When wattlebirds insist, I rise,
to lurch through morning matters.
As pigeons, flushed from ancient coops,
snap like cheap plastic bunting
and shit on idlers by the Institute,
I saunter down my local tributary
to join the human stream.

Dinks stroll, dykes cruise,
and, jetsam of the mental health regime,
derros shunt sad on this conveyor belt
between denim hills and the sea.

Outside Lucette's the faithful break focaccia,
take latte eucharist.
Two post-punk women lean across a table,
joined at the nose rings.
A Doberman jets chardonnay on chalkboard.

After bruschetta *agape* or catholic fish and chips
a breeze resuscitates me. On the sand
the parafoils inflate their nine-celled lungs
and New Age honeycomb takes flight like bees.

Night Game: World Cup 2002

The angel on the clocktower
is tired of marking time.
She heads a white ball to the rimming hills –
a full moon with no logo and no flag.

Taperoo Inventory

Slung between Norfolk Island pines
the ranges' endless hammocks.
Chimney stacks and radio masts
prop the canvas of the sky.
Above the dunes a kestrel whets the air,
foiled profile pure as steel.
On marram, spinifex and spurge
– the dune's green pelt –
galahs convene.

Along the shore, pinsqueaks of oystercatchers,
pipes of masked lapwings
rehearse for Carnevale
with strut and mince.

At the horizon's absolute
a yacht's nib signs its name
on the blank cheque of the sky.

Over the gulf a Cessna drones
Gregorian antiphons from twin Doppler throats –
Lauds and Magnificat for St Vincent's Day.

The Liturgy of the Leafy Sea Dragon

Ave, Sygnathidae,
et Phycodurus eques.
Heraldic in your hideaway,
All your servants sing your praise.
May your grace be with us.
Dominus in fishdom.

Fronded fretwork in freefall,
Ora pro nobis.
Cryptic in kelp, render us help,
Equus maris bogus.
Subtle on our seagrass plains
– looping leafage, local range –
Gloria in profundis.
We'll research you half to death
If some rich mug will fund us.

Mary at Nazareth
Didn't know what hit her
After meeting Gabriel,
Yet she wasn't bitter.
Took on single pregnancy;
Stigma, shame and infamy
Grew with every breath.

Ave, Sygnathidus!
You're a single parent.
This time it's the man who pays,
Brooding eggs for forty days
In Zostera and Posidonia.
Lord, have mercy on you!
Eaten by a ray, son.
Kyrie eleison!

Ave, Sygnathidus!
Dolphins are so passe.
Let's dispense with theme park fuss
And sing aquatic Angelus.

Siphon flute-mouth, golden eye,
Gloria! Alleluia!
Leafy dragon sweet and shy,
all our praise is due you.
Ave, Sygnathidus!
Morning starfish praise thee.
Te laudamus, little one.
You will drive us crazy!

Eco-freaks with bonsai brains,
Kneeling till our knees hurt,
We pour poison down our drains
But we've bought the T-shirt.

Notes
The Leafy Sea Dragon, *Phycodurus eques*,
belongs to the Sygnathidae (seahorse) family.
The males brood the fertilised eggs and give
birth to as many as 200 young.
Zostera and *Posidonia* are seagrass species.

Rejection Slip

Three points, two and a half, two,
three, three and a half,
three, three.

You stamped in your hurdle.
You were back from the end of the board.
You leaned too far forward.
Your takeoff was low.
Your flight path was flat.
Your degree of difficulty was too high.

You clipped the board with your fingers.
You frightened the judges.

Your tuck was too loose.
Your feet came apart in the third somersault.
We don't like the cut of your Speedos,
and green's not your colour.

You were
short/
long/
flat on your face/
your entry was vertical
but
you threw up a splash.
We expect you to rip it.

The judges from Sweden and Mexico
noticed a twist on the entry.

You bled on the tip of the springboard and
          into the pool.
It doesn't look good on TV.
You've been edited out.

Three points, two and a half, two,
three, three and a half,
three, three.

II

Field Notes

Drop Zone, Lower Light

High over Lower Light
flatland is lensed with blue
that magnifies its message,
focuses stubble-and-limestone paddocks,
the sloughed skin of the river,
the flywhisk pepper trees
that sheep have basin-cut.

Our jumpship bucks in thermals
above fawn plains, boxed, stapled.
From scalloped mangrove coast
the sea veins in.

At exit height.
The ruched Gulf in the breeze.
Beneath coarse-bristled pelt
faint relict dunes rib the peninsula
with phantom stripes, thylacine memories
that stir beneath a newer history.
Strut-hanger in the gale, a paper doll,
I join the count, release,
grip-change and spin in skyplay.

Break, track, deploy.
My canopy explodes
like gunfire from the army proving range.

And as I go to ground
cryptic quail flurry and rage,
erupt before my feet.

Kayak Surfing, Southern Fleurieu

On morning's mercury, that slick cloud-mirror,
the wind has pitched its tents.
The offshore leans on green walls,
curved spine against the waves
to tamp their mould.

Torn seagrass pennons stream.
A seabreeze scrawls graffiti on the glass.
Its catspaws rake the face,
but lose their grip, are gone.
The land breeze wins again.

My yellow kayak bucks.
I spoon salt water backward
and snap to face the shore.
Spume ghosts my sight.

A wave tugs at the stern
to winch it up the face.

I windmill forward, spurt
and ride the rail.
With lean and carve and slash
I peel, outwit whitewater,
and when I swivel seaward
another hollow wave sits up to beg.

Grey Mangroves

Green almonds of the sea,
we plump despite lean winter.
When the joyful gravity of spring
evicts us from our family tree,
we sail down tidal creeks,
shipwreck on siren mudflats.
We split our winter coats,
drop corkscrew anchors, brazen out
the tide that reams the creek.
Live graphs, we grow upon
a grid of snorkel roots
and chart our own statistics for survival.

Antiphon
After Lewis Thomas, The lives of a cell.

An ant, alone, has little on his mind.
Sparse neurons on a string aren't mind at all
and can't conspire to generate a thought.
He's just a ganglion on legs. And yet
ten ants around a dead moth on a path
clot into thought, cohere to an idea.
Shove, fumble, shunt. Their moth-meal moves uphill
as if by chance. But when you watch the press
of thousands on the anthill's blackened earth –
it's then you start to see the entity
emerge from roiling Rorschach, and observe
the logic of its great organic plan.
Nature's computer, programmed to survive,
each ant a byte, a crawling bit of wit.

Humpbacks Fishing

You blow like thermal vents
and head-butt daylight
to trap the writhe and thrash of mackerel
in your bubble-net lasso.

Wild wire whips, spools. The school
spins like a catherine wheel,
arcs silver like a rhythmic gymnast's ribbon.
But all its world is whale.

Accordioned, your pleated throats
balloon like trypots with their load
and squeeze it tight like bellows.

Then, submarines made flesh, you slide,
sink like lost continents. Sea-skin
heals seamlessly above you, seals
songs, transmitted tribally:
the notes of squeaky rubber toys,
the syrup-speech of saxophones,
the purity of a glass harmonica.

Liquid Paper

It's always had the jump on Gutenberg and Caxton,
this tidal printing press,
rolling out its liquid latest
twice daily round the planet.

Beyond the grasp of the barons
of bullshit and sleaze
and the headline SHARK RAPES NUN!
we read simplicities.

Retreating tide marks sand
with scallops and sines.
Shellgrit prints the braille edition
I read with my bare feet.

A seismographic trace of shells
graphs zig-zags on the beach –
ECGs of the sea.

The night edition's never put to bed,
and though streetlights at evening
barcode its graphite gloss,
no billionaire can ever buy it out.

Planetary tug-of-war
creates this palimpsest.

The rising tide will wipe the slate.

Thylacine

I am the striped totem
of this flayed island.
Naked in the westerlies,
torn by the Roaring Forties,
I clawed the beaten earth.
You flung me to the void.

You froze me in a snapshot.
A mangy ghost you made me:
a celluloid spectre,
torpid in a zoo.

You sold my pelt at auction
in Sotheby's and Christie's:
a curio for Croesus,
a merkin for his ego.

You stole my foetal young
to swell your pickled archive.
Today you gouge their genes;
you dredge their DNA
and ask, *Shall these bones live?*

I haunt the night of rumour;
I stalk the dark of history.
I sip stars and planets
from the billabong's bowl.
But the new moon hooks me;
the full moon chokes me.
You cut me from my island.
I cannot sing my dreaming.

I walk
with the last Vatican eunuch.

The last
light horseman.

The
last
dodo.

Notes for a Field Guide

I Wings

1 Galahs, Largs Bay
Sad, comma-headed Leunig clowns,
you clump to graze on dunes,
compact, absorbed, assiduous,
a troop of vagrant tribal hoons.

2 Pelican, Barker Inlet
Trundling
in a nil-wind launch,
slide-rise,
row low.
Tip-skim your own reflection.
Arc in air meets arc below.
Stroke on towards infinity
where curve above clips curve of sea
in the wake of your great bill-paunch.

3 Little Black Cormorants

Black cormorants in flight,
spill from your broken string
in knots and chains and skeins
and kite-tails wavering.

Fluting lines, morsing vee,
casually scored for a symphony,
you're silent, but you sing.

4 Red-capped Dotterels,
   Semaphore Beach

Dotterels at Semaphore
heliograph and Doppler,
morse and re-morse.
In dotterel dressage,
medium is message.

5 The Cry
Sharp as a squeaking hinge,
dry as a comb's teeth tweaked –
the lone note of a gull.

6 Sooty Oystercatchers
Red-masked men in black,
cloak-and-dagger birds
parting the curtain.

II Water

1 Sea Anemones
Discs in the rockpools:
sliced kiwi fruit,
iris of an eye.
Sand-floured in shallows,
faint negatives survive –
ghosts of a halo,
eyelashed and tonsured.

2 Sea Change
The sea is a flat blue desktop.
The terns that dive to click on instinct's icon
open the dolphin folder.

3 Relic

Cuttlebone, your owner's gone,
but I have his fingerprint
in swirling solenoids
and microscopic terraces.
Forensic tease, he never sensed his end,
but left this souvenir to lead me on.

III Bushed

1 Tawny Frogmouth
Snake-headed, lichened,
cryptic in the redgum,
the freeze-framed tawny frogmouth.

2 Magpie
A casual philanthropist,
the magpie, infinitely rich,
peels notes from his wad.

3 Welcome Swallow

Scissoring for insects,
terrain-following aircraft,
swallow and shadow connect.

4 Spiderweb

suspended,
you swinger,
grooved like a silver record
spun by a small DJ.
Every day a new hit.

5 Caterpillar

Fat, hairy concertina,
I tried to make you face the music
but you wriggled out of it.

6 Frill-necked Lizard

Jurassic parachute deployed,
transparently defiant,
the frill-necked lizard rears.

7 Cryptic

You have been in my mind for months, unwritten,
sunning yourself in marram on the dune:
rough bark on rotting wood,
dotted with yellow lichen.

Your tracks in flour-white sand
lead to a blunted double arrowhead:
stumpy-tailed lizard
placing an each-way bet.

Tree Fern

Coiled catherine wheel,
my fuse burns fierce in rain.
I brandish clenched brown fists,
compel you to my shadow puppet show.
I'm boxing glove, ruched seahorse and furled foetus,
coiled millipede, shillelagh, Viking prow.

In green epiphany
I flaunt new fronds, uncurl
brash as a party whistle in your face.
Fretwork, my paper doily templates
focus and etch the sun,
spray crisp graffiti on stream-sanded rock.
I gesture to seamed coal,
to ancient peat
pressed in Gondwana's steam. I fuse
geology to greenhouse-dotted suburbs.

Muster

The lost sounds gather on the shores of sleep,
shuffle together, lower woolly heads,
drink deep, confer,
discreet as undertakers.

Branches, like snares, brush roofing iron.
Weatherboards creak, confide in cracked, decrepit voices.
A harvest train sings down the line.
Doors swing and squeak;
the house moves in its dreams. A kelpie snores.
Windsong rings its bell,
and wreathes this wooden box. The clock
herds tinny history
and musters us for sleep.

Played Out

Old audiotapes, near death,
retire to Adelaide's beaches
with their redundant songs.
They mourn lost comrades smashed in car parks
or wound on wheels of cars,
then play out their last moments.

They clump in condominiums,
ribboned sculptures,
wave-rounded, sodden shaggy dogs,
old haystacks walled along the high tide mark.
And, chopped at last to tealeaf slurry,
their music minced to solitary notes,
die with no swan song.

Tapas

1 Eroti-con
Sex on the Internet? Ten out of ten!
The real thing is no go.
Live vicariously, then
Buy the video.

2 The Physics Exam
If gravity holds the universe together
who wants the last laugh?

3 A Postmodern Prayer
Thank God
for the secular state.

4 Pebble
Story
of
Everest
and
time.

5 Stobie Pole

Totem of our treeless state.
Felled, a narrow-gauge railway
designed by a committee.

6 Milk Jug

Houri, veiled and beaded,
you danced before Pasteur.

7 Corkscrew
I see right through your empty head,
squeeze your waiting arms.
You're always ready to screw.

8 Walnut
Vegetable skull.
Concussed, your brain is manna.

9 Simile
Workshopping a poem
is like
faking an orgasm.

Drop

Crystal pear, I stretch
the sac of my meniscus.
I spider-swing from the spout,
fine-blown glass.
Pinched finally from my stem,
I bow to gravity, launch my

f
r
e
e
f
a
l
l,

create the bullseye that I hit,
shatter like a lightbulb.

To Celia: an apostrophe upon a comma

Commas can be an emotional experience.
Celia Jellett, Editor, 9 May 2000

Twos with docked tails, sad-eyed,
wag bleeding stumps.
Despite abuse, they're keen to please,
and hang upon my words.

Constrained
by the minimal comma policy,
they stand ready to serve
even the shortest sentence.

Desperate for work,
they queue for every vacancy.

Masochists,
they prefer a long term with hard labour
to a suspended sentence.

But life holds tender moments. Paired,
they spurn the missionary position,
adopt the fretwork curlicues
of a snuggled sixty nine.

They shrivel, after cometary climax,
to headphones, earmuffs, sagging vinyl beanbags,
beached jelly-blubber magnifying sand,
then blow great post-coital Os of smoke,
talk of religion and philosophy,
and know whatever credo they embrace
will be forever quoted.

III

I Took the Words Right Out of
Your Mouth

The River Children
After Seamus Heaney

When we lay on the jarrah planks
Riverlight flicked through splintered cracks
Green slivers into our eyes.

High sun and lunchtime whistles agreed on noon
And the land breeze freighted smells
Of flour mills, sawn pine, sour tanneries.

We knew nothing then of death
Though salt stiffened on our skins
And suntime frayed our telomeres.

That year before TV
When thongs first slapped our streets
Mimicking rain in drought

Our world was wharf and water,
Tin changerooms, oildrum rafts
In the gut of a gritty port

Where the shuttling *Karatta* and *Yandra*
Laced Adelaide to the outports,
Weaving the gulfs together.

Baptised in salt and Speedos,
Proddy and Mick were allies.
We shed our sects with our clothes,

And shared sly cigarettes
By the Jervois Bridge and the Sugar Wharf
Where the refinery puffed its steel havana.

For we knew that our tribal gibes
Were only fit for schooltime, rain
And mothballed winter coats.

Donne's Condom

Ere that I lay mee down a-bed,
Ere that owre love wee consummate,
Lest shee shall bee undone by Donne
When shee shall think it all in funne,
My condom shall I don.

I stand enclosed in latex caul.
Let the sunne's beames not shine at all
On mee and shee I cherish,
For what shall stay my mistress' fall,
Alas, if rubber perish?

Each atomie and molecule
Unites in heavenly tension still.
Let no man but a knave or foole
Await the coming of the Pill.

Variation on a Theme of Emily Dickinson

Irritation – is the walking –
Of a dog beside the sea
And launching – from my hand – a sphere –
High and ballistically –

And finding that – when canine teeth
Make ultimate connection –
The orb has dropped into the brine
Despite – my firm direction

And that I must remove my shoes
From pedal installation –
And fetch the fucking ball myself –
And suffer marination.

The Blue Crane

The bird is my neighbour, a whimsical fellow and dim;
There is in the lake a nobility falling on him.
John Shaw Neilson, *The Crane is My Neighbour*

Elegant Audrey Hepburn bird,
anorexic dancer,
why did Shaw Neilson call you 'he'?
I can't provide an answer.

Discreet and svelte and feminine
beneath the mangroves' shade,
I know there must be boys as well,
or how did you get made?

'Sexes alike,' the field guides say.
You're all as fair as Venus,
but underneath that feathered grey
somebody's got a penis.

The Obsession of Ethel Malley

The letter sits unfinished on the table.
The kitchen scales weigh out the afternoon.
The clockface sifts the daylight into minutes.
Light music from a mantel radio
sprinkles the air with jitterbug that fills
the purple cyclamen's reflected cup.
A blowfly kneads its treacle feet in sugar,
and peppers it, and leaves.

                                 A tuba farts.
The Salvos march redemptive down the street,
naked except for begging bowls and bonnets.
The Sacred Heart above the mantel hangs
in anatomical absurdity,
and Ethel wears her heart upon her sleeve.

Ern Malley's corpse lies in a cypress coffin,
his poems on his chest. His sister weeps,
reflects how manticore and stiff demotic
snuffed his green fuse too soon. She takes her pen,
recharged with blue Onoto, blots her tears,
completes her letter to the editor,
proffers the evidence of genius.

'Dear Mr Harris,
                    May I call you Max?

'The cockatoo you raped at Pinky Flat
objects to your perversion. Publish these
and I shall be discreet. Solicitors
shall go without their fees. Ern's fantasies
drift like slow ships upon a brew of dreams,
slide like tectonic plates on olive oil,
or slugs on double cream. Snare the black swan
     of trespass,
and flora from my brother's ruptured gut
shall fertilise a dozen angry penguins,
and he shall live forever.
                   Ethel Malley'

Antarctic Skydiving
Allergy after John Forbes

When the equable climate of Bali is not what it was
& your spirits drop harder than coconuts bombing
      blancmange
& namedropping gets you fuckall & nowhere
& you've lost all your faith in the balm of the
      tropical air
then it's time for Antarctic skydiving.

Pack your gear & a Mars bar.
You'll never know such relief
as you l& at Mawson base
        in your Speedos & parka

boarding the jumpship for
a night dive from ten gr&,
the door off, the slip-
        stream tempered steel

& you & all the crew
slashed by razor wind
through the stashed Marvel comics
        that make or mar mind

but never matter. Fill up
your ration pack in case
you stuff the exit point
        & need a pickup

or a lorry. Somebody
just dug in. Bolt on
into that sessile phone
        box. Dial a mayday.

Four heads on ice
wish you were here
in freefall with speed
        like a dozing shark

or the mind of a stone draped
in the planet's luminous
substrate on a beach
        with a girl from Sydney.

Pussy
After Kate Llewellyn

he sits in Swains
with his lover
forks moules marinieres
and tongues them

he strolls in the conservatory
fingers a Venus flytrap
and drools

he snorkels over fields
of sea anemones
with wanting mouths
and fringing cilia
and dreams

sometimes he eats mushroom
and cucumber salad
so she won't know
he's obsessed

but she eats sausages
bites bananas
licks Magnums

he can't fool her

After Dorothy Porter

I visit the greengrocer
from Crete.

I heft a watermelon
fondle its firm skin

salivate
        diamonds
of
        languor and lust.

Cleave me, Lady,
it urges.

Its green breast
swells
as I watch.

My lips pout,
part
like your thighs
on the beach by the wine-dark sea
in the Cretan night.

Your juices madden me.

I stab.

We
both
fall
apart.

Takin' the Piss
After Geoff Goodfellow

i was in the Federal
last pay day
sinkin' a few
when in comes that loud runt
– y' know what that rhymes with –
& starts yellin' at us
don't call me lad, dad –

bullshit

shortarsed wanker
everybody knows
y' gotta keep yr kids in line

kev & me
come in
f'r a quiet beer
& this little arsehole's roarin'
at the top of his voice
'e shoulda stood on the jetty
we still coulda heard 'im

fucken poser
gave us all the shits
so i grabbed 'is beer
& baptised 'im.

takin' the piss   areya?   i sez
well   more than one
c'n play that game
& by the way   mate
tell me
do you like sex & travel?
cos if y' do   y' c'n

fuck

      off

After Federico Garcia Lorca

Blue snow on No-Name Pass
bled in the sun.
A brook, a freshet
flushed the mountain's ducts.
In Dolorosa Valley
blue eyes – Gemelos Lakes.
At a brimming pool
I drink your tears, Luisa.

Ode to Garcia Lorca

The poet on stilts
rides his pogo stick proudly.
He saddles his steed,
Jackhammer the donkey.
His motive is loco.
He sacks the Alhambra
and pisses from steeples.
His woman so wooden
and high-strung and waisted
plays on him and for him
the songs of Segovia.

Mummy
After Sylvia Plath

Mummy, I'm unwinding you.
You're ancient Egyptian, not Jew.
You're so tight-wound and pure,
A coiled armature.
Mummy, I'm unwinding you.

Mummy, I'm undressing you,
You matron of natron and glue.
You've no heart and no brain
And no blood in your veins.
Mummy, I'm undressing you.

Mummy, you're gutted, you're past it,
You miserable middle-class bastard.
But at least you're beyond getting plastered
On bourbon, martinis and daiquiris
While Jews boil to glue in your factories.

You crushed me beneath suede stilettos.
I was bruised and abused and reviled,
Your Polish-American child.
You bitch in your pearls and twinset. Oh!
You locked me away in a ghetto.

Mummy, you're fully unwound.
Your bones shall return to the ground.

I shall pound them with pestle and mortar,
Your dutiful, houseproud daughter.
Mummy, you're fully unwound.
Mummy, you're dust on the ground.

I shall give you and daddy short shrift:
You both read my poems and sniffed.
When I write my next prize-winning poem
My pen-name shall be Hannah J Baum,
For my verse is uniquely my gift.

Mummy, don't phone me or email.
You stifled me, elderly female.
Vile vampire, I'm so glad you're dead!
It's settled: I'm marrying Ted.
Stay away, stay away from our bed!

The Temperature of Neoprene
After Wallace Stevens

Surf the rollers beneath the stars,
My muscular one. Launch from the lip,
Carve cutbacks. *Don't drop in, you turds!*
Let the tench's caudal fin regress
And drag along the sand; and mind the buoys,
For hit one, stoned, and you'll be in the papers.
Let midnight tubes be green.
The ambient temperature is the temperature of neoprene.

Make from the skins of seals,
When you've removed their knobs, a seat
That you can park your fanny on.
Now spread it so as to cover her face.
If she's horny, let her come
But first remove her bubble gum.
Your wetsuit crotch has burst its seam.
The ambient temperature is the temperature of neoprene.

Organ Voluntary

After William Carlos Williams

I have eaten
the heart and lungs
that were in
the esky

and which
you had probably
earmarked
for transplant

and destined
for a colleague
who smoked
all his life

I ate them raw
they were delicious
fresh-killed
and so cold

serves him right
cretin
physician
heal thyself

Acknowledgements

John Couper-Smart and Christine Courtney, *Port Adelaide: Tales from a Commodious Harbour*; Cathy Young (ed.), *Beyond the Shimmering: the Gawler Literary Fund Anthology*; *Beyond Ben Bulben*; *The Bunyip*; *Friendly Street Reader 27*; *Sidewalk*; *Yellow Moon*; PoeticA, ABC Radio 891, Radio 5UV.

My thanks to Roger Zubrinich and Mike Ladd from the Adelaide Institute of TAFE (Professional Writing Unit) for their excellent teaching and guidance, to Graeme Webster, my poetry teacher at Hamilton Adult Campus, to Friendly Street Poets, and to Heather Knight and Mary and John McKenzie, intelligent poetry readers from the real world.